JOE **BIDEN**

46th US President

BY RYAN GALE

CONTENT CONSULTANT
RACHEL BLUM, PhD
DEPARTMENT OF POLITICAL SCIENCE
UNIVERSITY OF OKLAHOMA

Essential Library

An Imprint of Abdo Publishing | abdobooks.com

abdobooks.com

Published by Abdo Publishing, a division of ABDO, PO Box 398166, Minneapolis, Minnesota 55439. Copyright © 2021 by Abdo Consulting Group, Inc. International copyrights reserved in all countries. No part of this book may be reproduced in any form without written permission from the publisher. Essential Library™ is a trademark and logo of Abdo Publishing.

Printed in the United States of America, North Mankato, Minnesota.
102020
012021

THIS BOOK CONTAINS
RECYCLED MATERIALS

Cover Photo: Matt Rourke/AP Images
Interior Photos: Andrew Harnik/AP Images, 4, 95; Evan Vucci/AP Images, 8, 85; Carolyn Kaster/AP Images, 10, 88; AP Images, 12, 39; Auk Archive/Alamy, 17; Joseph Sohm/Shutterstock Images, 19; Rob Carr/AP Images, 20; Slim Aarons/Getty Images, 24; Shutterstock Images, 27; Real Window Creative/Shutterstock Images, 31; Bettmann/Getty Images, 33, 37, 42; Mark Reinstein/MediaPunch/IPX/AP Images, 45; George Widman/AP Images, 49; John Duricka/AP Images, 51; Photographer's Mate 1st Class Arlo K. Abrahamson/US Navy, 57; Charles Dharapak/AP Images, 59; Charlie Neibergall/AP Images, 60; Alex Brandon/AP Images, 64; Elise Amendola/AP Images, 67; Jacquelyn Martin/AP Images, 68; Khalid Mohammed/AP Images, 72; Mel Evans/AP Images, 77; Susan Walsh/AP Images, 78; Kyodo/AP Images, 80; Patrick Semansky/AP Images, 92

Editor: Arnold Ringstad
Series Designer: Becky Daum

Library of Congress Control Number: 2020940290

Publisher's Cataloging-in-Publication Data

Names: Gale, Ryan, author.
Title: Joe Biden: 46th US President / by Ryan Gale
Other title: 46th US President
Description: Minneapolis, Minnesota : Abdo Publishing, 2021 | Series: Essential lives | Includes online resources and index
Identifiers: ISBN 9781532194108 (lib. bdg.) | ISBN 9781098213466 (ebook)
Subjects: LCSH: Biden, Joseph R., Jr.--Juvenile literature. | Legislators--United States --Biography.--Juvenile literature. | Presidents--United States--Biography.--Juvenile literature.
Classification: DDC 973.933--dc23

CONTENTS

CHAPTER
ONE

LIGHT IN THE DARKNESS

The lights went up in a dark room, revealing a man standing behind a podium with a backdrop of American flags. The front of the wooden podium read "D20." The date was August 20, 2020. It was the finale of the 2020 Democratic National Convention (DNC), and the man was Joe Biden, the Democratic party nominee for president of the United States.

The room was completely silent. Then Biden began to speak. He described the political, economic, and racial strife that was engulfing the nation as a battle between darkness and light. The country was in the midst of the coronavirus pandemic, which had sickened millions around the world, killed hundreds of thousands of Americans, and caused the worst economic crisis since the Great Depression of the 1930s. Biden said that the country was beset by social, racial, and environmental injustice, and he charged that President

Joe Biden's speech at the 2020 DNC gave him a chance to pitch his candidacy to the nation in the closing months of the campaign.

Donald Trump and his administration were ineffectual and corrupt. This was the darkness Biden alluded to. But he proclaimed, "If you entrust me with the presidency, I will draw on the best of us, not the worst. I will be an ally of the light, not of the darkness."[1]

In his speech, Biden accepted the Democratic presidential nomination and then outlined how he planned to fix the nation's many problems. His plan involved getting the pandemic under control, getting kids safely back to school, creating jobs in manufacturing, improving the health-care and education systems, dealing with climate change, and fighting racism. This was Biden's metaphorical light.

THE CORONAVIRUS

The coronavirus first appeared in Wuhan, China, in late 2019, and it spread to more than 170 countries, killing hundreds of thousands of people and sickening millions within months.[2] The first US case was discovered in late January 2020. President Trump at first denied that the virus was a threat, and he took few actions to slow its spread until March. The United States soon had more coronavirus cases than any other country in the world. At the time of the 2020 Democratic National Convention, more than 170,000 Americans had died from the virus.[3]

An Experienced Candidate

Biden announced his bid for president in April 2019. He saw himself as the best Democratic candidate to beat Republican incumbent president Donald Trump. Trump was a businessman with no political experience prior to his 2016 election. He had run in that campaign as an antiestablishment candidate who said his business experience would give him a perspective on managing the country that career politicians didn't have. Even so, his presidency saw political divisiveness, scandals, and impeachment. When Biden entered the race, there were already more than a dozen Democratic candidates who were eager to defeat Trump. Biden eventually shot ahead as the front-runner.

Biden had a wealth of political experience. He had been a politician for more than forty years, first as a county councilman, then as a senator for the state of Delaware, and later as vice president in the administration of President Barack Obama. Biden had also run for president twice before, once in the 1988 election and again in the 2008 election, but he had been unsuccessful. Biden drew on his experience and the

A large field of Democratic candidates sought to unseat incumbent president Donald Trump.

lessons he learned from his two previous campaigns to finally win the Democratic Party nomination in 2020.

A Difficult Campaign

Biden had many obstacles to face in order to win the election. He had an uphill battle in defeating an incumbent president. Unseating an incumbent can be a difficult task, as the sitting president has many advantages, such as name recognition, an established base of financial donors, and a national platform from which to readily reach the American people. In the previous ten elections with incumbent candidates, only three incumbents had lost.

VIRTUAL DNC

Political conventions have historically been large events with numerous speakers, live music, and thousands of supporters. But the 2020 DNC was different. Large gatherings were considered unsafe during the coronavirus pandemic, so the 2020 convention was a virtual event. The convention was broadcast on news channels for two hours a night between August 17 and 20, which made it significantly shorter than most previous conventions. The broadcasts contained both live and prerecorded speeches and musical performances. Notable speakers included former secretary of state Hillary Clinton, Vermont senator Bernie Sanders, and former presidents Bill Clinton and Barack Obama.

Biden gave his acceptance speech at the Chase Center in Delaware, with only a handful of reporters in the room. The applause that followed his speech came from a series of television monitors placed around the stage that displayed live broadcasts of a select few supporters. Afterward, Biden and his wife, Jill, went outdoors to view fireworks. The Bidens and a small gathering of spectators wore face masks and remained safe distances apart to prevent the spread of the virus. Some political commentators felt that party conventions might never be the same after the 2020 DNC, as many Americans see large, lengthy conventions as expensive and outdated.

The 2020 campaign was marked by visible signs of the ongoing pandemic, such as face masks.

The 2020 election was also not a typical election. The pandemic made traveling and holding public campaign events difficult, as large gatherings were discouraged in order to prevent the spread of the virus.

Biden had to find alternate ways to reach the American people, such as by holding virtual events from his home studio and speaking to donors and supporters via telephone and video conferences. He had run in elections in every decade since the 1970s, but the 2020 presidential election was likely the most complex and challenging race of Biden's life.

AN ESTABLISHMENT POLITICIAN

Some people labeled Biden an establishment politician. *Establishment* is an ambiguous word that can mean different things to different people. It can mean someone who has spent a lifetime in politics, or it can mean a member of the political elite. It can mean someone who supports the current state of things. It can refer to a moderate politician, or one who avoids extreme positions on issues. Or it can mean a mainstream politician whose politics align with those of the majority of Americans. Politicians often seek to avoid being known as establishment politicians. Politicians with extreme views on issues, or those that go against the norm, are sometimes labeled antiestablishment.

CHAPTER
TWO

A NATURAL LEADER

Joseph Robinette Biden Jr. was born in the coal mining town of Scranton, Pennsylvania, on November 20, 1942. Joe, or Joey, as his parents called him, was named after his father, Joseph Robinette Biden Sr. His mother, Catherine Eugenia Finnegan Biden, had grown up in Scranton and met Joe Sr. in high school, shortly after his family moved there from Wilmington, Delaware. The couple married in May of 1941.

Joe Sr. worked for his uncle's manufacturing company during World War II (1939–1945), and he was put in charge of its operations in Boston, Massachusetts. Once he had saved enough money, he decided to go into business for himself. But when his business failed, the Bidens were forced to move in with Catherine's parents in Scranton. Work was scarce in Scranton, so for the next year Joe Sr. commuted more than 100 miles (160 km) to Wilmington, where he cleaned boilers for a heating and air-conditioning company.

Scranton was a working-class mining town in the 1940s, and Joey Biden had a working-class upbringing.

A Typical Childhood

Joey's childhood was typical of a boy living in a working-class family in the late 1940s and 1950s. He played with his younger siblings, James, Frank, and Val. He went to the movie theater, played baseball and football in the streets with his friends, and got into mischief around town. Joey was small for his age and had a stutter that he was self-conscious about, but he was

THE WORKING CLASS

Joey's father was among the millions of working-class, or blue-collar, Americans. The working class is the lowest of the three socioeconomic classes that group people with similar economic, educational, or social statuses. Working-class people usually have jobs that do not require college education, such as laborer, farmer, mechanic, and salesperson. People in the middle class, called white-collar workers, have jobs that require higher education, such as manager, academic, engineer, lawyer, doctor, and civil servant. The upper class has the highest status and the greatest wealth, and it represents the smallest of the three classes. People in this class may own successful companies or make money from investments. For many Americans, a key goal in life has long been to make their way into a higher class.

In the early 1950s, the labor force in the United States was mostly made up of blue-collar workers, but that began to change throughout the decade. In 1944, President Franklin D. Roosevelt had signed the GI bill, which gave grants to World War II veterans so they could attend college or trade schools. As a result, in the years after the war, many Americans received higher education, got well-paying jobs, and entered the middle class. In the late 1950s, white-collar workers outnumbered blue-collar workers for the first time.

tough and a natural leader. Looking back years later, his childhood friend Tommy Bell said he was "an aggressive guy, he was a leader, he was a risk-taker. He was a good guy."[1]

Joey was surrounded by family at his Scranton home and learned many important things from them that shaped the rest of his life. Later in life, he said his father taught him the value of hard work, his mother taught him humility and how to be just, and his grandfather taught him about honesty and equality. He learned about sports and politics listening to his grandfather and uncles, who spent many lively evenings talking and debating around the kitchen table.

Archmere

When Joey was ten, his family moved north of Wilmington to be closer to his father's workplace. From his bedroom window in the family's new apartment, Joey could see Archmere. It was a beautiful mansion and estate built by

THE FINNEGANS

Joey spent much of his early childhood among his mother's family, the Finnegans, and visited them often later in life. Unlike his father's family, the Finnegans had college educations. But there was also a history of alcoholism among the Finnegans, for which reason Joey never drank alcohol as an adult.

businessman John J. Raskob in Claymont, Delaware, and it had been turned into a private Catholic preparatory school, Archmere Academy. Joey's parents were Catholic, and they raised him in the Catholic faith and enrolled him in Catholic schools. Joey got a closer view of the school when his Catholic Youth Organization football team was allowed to practice there. He wanted nothing else but to attend the exclusive Archmere.

When the time came to look for a high school, Joey tried to convince his parents to send him to Archmere, but his dad balked at the $300 annual tuition.[2] His dad tried to talk him into attending other, less expensive schools, but Joey found his way in when he learned that Archmere had a work-study program. After passing the entrance exam, he spent the summer before his freshman year working on the school grounds weeding gardens, washing windows, and painting.

Joey's first day at Archmere in September 1957 was like a dream come true. He got off the school bus wearing a new suit and tie and gazed at the gardens, the elm trees that ran down to the Delaware River, and the elegant Archmere mansion. But things didn't go quite the way he had dreamed they would. He was one of the smallest kids in his class, and his fellow students mocked

Joey's time at Archmere was filled with learning and growth.

him because he had a stutter. But by the end of his time there, he had grown significantly, become a popular student, and proved himself to be a gifted athlete. He had also become a student leader, and he was voted class president his junior and senior years. When a friend's father asked teenage Joey what he wanted to do when he was older, he said he wanted to be president of the United States, and no one questioned it.

Overcoming an Obstacle

Joey's stutter loomed over him like a dark cloud throughout his childhood. He was fine when at home among family and friends, but his stutter would appear when he was in new or stressful situations. Joey was mocked by classmates and even teachers, and he often

GIVE ME THE BALL

Joey was a natural athlete, and he played baseball, basketball, and football at school and for fun. He had a passion for sports, and he dreamed of playing professional football. He was fast, and he was the top scorer on the football team his senior year at Archmere. "I was always the kid who said, 'give me the ball,'" he recalled years later.[3] Joey's teammates called him Hands for his skill at catching footballs. He found confidence and acceptance in sports that he hadn't always found elsewhere.

had low self-confidence as a result. Joey avoided situations in which he would have to speak in public, and he memorized sentences to use in certain situations, such as when meeting new people or making small talk with neighbors. This helped him avoid stuttering.

When Joey was younger, his parents tried to help him overcome his stutter by sending him to a speech pathologist, but it didn't help. When he entered high school, Joey's teachers exempted him from having to speak in front of his classmates, but he didn't want to be treated differently. He worked as hard as he could to overcome his stutter. Joey memorized poems and then spent hours in front of a mirror reciting them. He forced himself to relax the muscles in his face that would tighten when he got nervous. In his sophomore year, Joey's stutter began to improve, and he started doing his public speaking assignments in front of his class.

Joe Biden overcame a childhood stutter to become an accomplished public speaker.

He was eventually able to overcome his stutter with the encouragement of his family and teachers, and he spoke in front of his graduating class in June 1961.

Later in life, he would look back on his stutter not as an impediment but as a builder of character. He wrote years later: "Carrying it strengthened me and . . . made me a better person. And the very things it taught me turned out to be invaluable lessons for my life as well as my chosen career."[4] Joey became increasingly talkative after overcoming his stutter. In his late twenties, he was described as a "compulsive talker" who, according to a colleague, "could give an extemporaneous 15-minute speech on the underside of a blade of grass."[5]

CHAPTER
THREE

FINDING HIS TRUE CALLING

B iden's father had insisted he go to college. No Biden had ever been to college, and his father regretted not getting a higher education himself. As a teenager, Biden had two aims for his future career path. One was to pursue his passion for sports and play professional football. The other was to "become an esteemed public figure—who would do great things and earn a place in the history books," as he would later recall.[1] Biden was a practical person and admitted that being a pro football player was a long shot. But he had skills that would be helpful in achieving his other goal.

Near the end of his junior year at Archmere, Biden picked up a book about Congress from the school library and flipped through the legislators' biographies. He wanted to know how the politicians had reached their high positions. Some, he read, had come from wealthy and well-connected families. Others had gotten there

Biden's studies at the University of Delaware shaped his future career. Decades later, he returned to the school for a 2008 campaign event.

on their own, and many of them had worked as lawyers before entering politics. Biden's family was not wealthy and had no political connections, so he decided at that moment to become a lawyer.

Biden was accepted to the University of Delaware in Newark, Delaware, and began taking classes in the fall of 1961. He planned to earn a double major in political science and history. Biden spent his first semester focusing on football after he made it onto the freshman team. But his grades suffered as a result, and his parents made him give up playing in order to concentrate on his classes. Biden still didn't fully apply himself to his studies. He knew what he wanted to do with his life, so he concentrated on the classes that would be useful to him and let the others slide. Instead of studying, he spent his time in the student lounge discussing politics, civil rights, and international affairs with his friends.

Biden's habits continued through his sophomore year, and he started his junior year with an unimpressive transcript. There was a chance his grades would not be good enough to get him accepted into law school, so he made a commitment to himself to turn things around. Biden took extra classes and moved off campus, where, according to his roommate Tom Lewis, "there was nothing to do but study."[2] His grades improved, and he began playing football again.

Neilia

In the spring of 1964, Biden and his friends traveled to Fort Lauderdale, Florida, for a spring break vacation. But Biden quickly tired of the

THE VIETNAM WAR

While Biden was in college, the United States was fighting in the Vietnam War (1954–1975) to stop the spread of communism. Biden was opposed to the war, not because he saw it as immoral but because he considered it "a horrendous waste of time, money, and lives based on a flawed premise."[3] Because he was a student, Biden was able to get a deferment that kept him from being drafted into the military and sent to Vietnam. Biden also had asthma, a medical condition that disqualified him from serving in the military, so he got a medical deferment after he graduated. Such deferments were common among men of Biden's generation. Some critics, pointing to Biden's active childhood, have suggested that his medical deferment was simply to avoid military service.

Biden met his future wife, Neilia Hunter, along the beach on the Bahamas' Paradise Island.

beach crowds, so he jumped at the opportunity for a change of scenery when a friend suggested they take a flight to Paradise Island in the Bahamas. The island was filled with college students, but Biden was drawn to a woman he saw sitting on the beach. She had blonde hair and green eyes. Biden introduced himself. "Hi, Joe," she replied, "I'm Neilia Hunter."[4]

Biden and Neilia fell into conversation naturally. He learned that she was a student at New York's Syracuse University and dreamed of being a schoolteacher. Biden asked her to go to dinner with him that evening, and she accepted. Biden had planned on spending only one day in the Bahamas, but he ended up staying four days, spending much of that time with Neilia. The two made plans to meet the following weekend at her family's home in Skaneateles, New York.

Every weekend, Biden drove the 320 miles (515 km) from Newark to Skaneateles to visit Neilia. That summer, he got a job at a marina in Skaneateles to be near her. He also gave up playing football his senior year at the University of Delaware so he would have the weekends free. The more time they spent together, the less they talked about the past and the more they talked about a possible future. Neilia planned to teach at an elementary school. Biden planned to finish his bachelor's degree and then start law school. They planned to get married and start a family. Biden would work as a trial lawyer, start his own law firm, and then run for public office. In the spring of 1965, Biden accomplished the first goal on his list—he graduated from the University of Delaware.

A New Life

Since Neilia was working as a teacher in Syracuse, Biden applied to law school at the Syracuse University College of Law. With decent test scores and glowing recommendations from his college professors, he was accepted and began in the fall of 1965. But he quickly fell back into his old routine. He didn't study and missed classes. Instead, he played touch football in an intramural league, went to social gatherings, and spent time with Neilia. It wasn't long before this had serious consequences.

Six weeks into his first term at law school, Biden failed to correctly cite a source in a paper he wrote for a technical writing class, and he was accused of plagiarism. He later admitted that he hadn't attended enough class to know the proper procedure. His case was brought before the faculty for judgment and possible punishment. The faculty members judged that while he had plagiarized, it had been an accident. They made Biden retake the course.

Neilia used her skills as a teacher to help Biden study, and he was able to make it through his first year of law school. Shortly after his first term ended, he and

Biden did not excel at Syracuse, but he did discover the interests that would guide his future political career.

Neilia got married in Skaneateles on August 27, 1966. Neilia's father was skeptical of Biden. The Hunters were Protestant, and Biden was Catholic. Her father also didn't like the fact that Biden had no money. But Neilia's father had faith in her, so he gave the marriage his blessing.

Back at school, Biden developed an interest in the US federal government and international law. He also developed a fondness for public speaking. While he didn't do well academically, Biden's law professors saw that he had the skills necessary to be a good lawyer. One of his professors, Thomas Maroney, would later recall thinking that Biden "might not wind up being the top student in his class but he was going to wind up as somebody someday."[5]

It is common for law students to work in the field before getting a law degree, and in the spring of 1968, Biden accepted a job in Wilmington at the law firm Prickett, Ward, Burt & Sanders. Biden would work as a law clerk until he passed the bar exam, which he needed to do to practice law. Biden graduated from law school shortly after accepting the job, and he and Neilia moved to Wilmington.

Prickett, Ward, Burt & Sanders was a well-known law firm that represented big companies in the oil, construction, and insurance industries. But Biden felt like these large companies, with their substantial resources, were trampling working-class people to save money. He left the firm after only six months.

In late 1968, Wilmington was still feeling the effects of riots stemming from the assassination of civil rights leader Martin Luther King Jr. the previous spring. During that time, Biden watched events unfold on the nightly news, and he felt that Black people were victimized by police and the government. He wanted to do something to help, so he applied to work at the public defender's office, where he could ensure that minorities who couldn't afford a lawyer got adequate legal representation.

Politics and Family

Biden was only able to get part-time work as a public defender, so he got a second part-time job at the law

THE WILMINGTON RIOTS

In the 1960s, the country was in the midst of the civil rights movement, during which Black people fought to end legalized racism and segregation in the United States. This was often done using nonviolent means, such as boycotts, sit-ins, and protests. Occasionally, events escalated into riots. When civil rights leader Martin Luther King Jr. was assassinated in April of 1968, riots broke out across the country, including in Wilmington. Rioters in Wilmington vandalized property, looted stores, and threw rocks and bottles at police officers. Local law enforcement officers were quickly overwhelmed, prompting Delaware governor Charles Terry to deploy the state's National Guard in the city.

Even after the riots had ended, Governor Terry kept the National Guard troops in place, fearing a resurgence. Armed soldiers continued patrolling predominantly Black neighborhoods. This ended only after Terry was replaced by the election of a new governor, who promptly withdrew the military forces. The occupation of Wilmington lasted nine months, making it the longest military occupation of an American city since the Civil War (1861–1865).

firm Arensen & Balick. His boss, Sid Balick, was considered one of the best criminal defense lawyers in Wilmington, and he taught Biden how to be a good lawyer. Balick was also active in local politics. He and Biden discussed political matters in their spare time, and he got Biden involved in the Democratic Forum, an organization set on reforming the Democratic Party in Delaware.

In 1970, Biden was approached by a member of the Democratic Forum who suggested that he run for the New Castle County councilman seat for his district. As a county councilman, Biden would help pass laws to improve county operations and the lives of its residents. Biden had little interest in the position. He was more interested in foreign affairs than local politics. He was also extremely busy. By that time, Biden and Neilia had two young children, first Joseph Robinette "Beau" Biden III, born February 3, 1969, and then Robert Hunter Biden, born February 4, 1970. By this time Biden had also passed the bar exam and was planning to start his own law firm. But Biden was eager to help the Democratic Party, and win or lose, he would gain valuable experience. Even if he did win, the council only met two nights a week, so the time commitment would

New Castle County includes Wilmington, Delaware's most populous city.

not be overwhelming. After talking it over with Neilia, he agreed to run.

Biden got his sister Val to manage his campaign. They had an uphill battle to fight, as the residents of his district were mainly Republican. However, the district was made up mostly of working-class neighborhoods like the one Biden had grown up in. He went door-to-door throughout the district and used his blue-collar roots to connect with people and swing their votes. "I knew how to talk to them," Biden recalled years later. "I understood they valued government and fiscal austerity."[6] To Biden's surprise, he won the county council seat in the November election by 2,000 votes out of more than 19,000 cast.[7] His political career was underway.

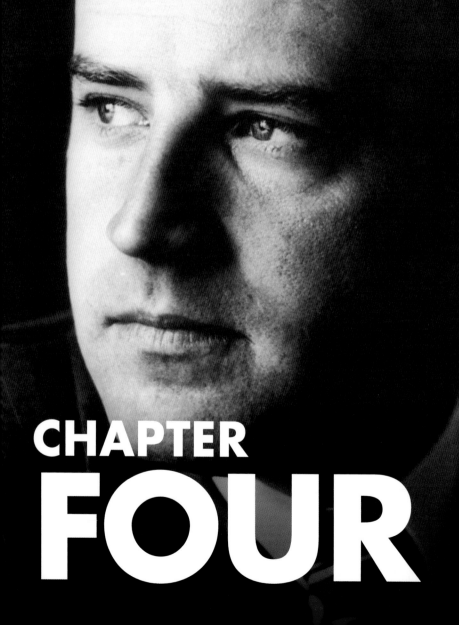

CHAPTER
FOUR

VICTORY AND LOSS

Biden threw himself into his work as a county councilman. He worked to reform tax laws, curb the aggressive expansion of oil companies, and cease construction of an unpopular highway. He developed a reputation as someone who would take on big industry and fight for the working class.

At the same time, Biden was testing the waters for a run for the US Senate to replace Republican senator James Caleb Boggs, who was up for reelection in 1972. As a senator, Biden could be involved in the issues he was passionate about, such as foreign affairs and civil rights. Biden discussed the idea with friends and fellow politicians. They responded with support, but they didn't think he had much chance of winning. They knew Biden had enthusiasm and drive, but Boggs was a popular senator who hadn't lost a statewide election since 1946. Regardless, Biden made up his mind to run.

During his tenure as a county councilman, Biden also had his eye on a higher office.

An Unwinnable Election

Though Biden had decided to run for Senate, he chose not to go public with his candidacy until he had a chance to begin building a voter base. From late 1971 through early 1972, Biden, with the help of his family, organized hundreds of receptions, coffee socials, and other gatherings around Delaware to win the support of voters. But he wasn't able to keep his campaign a secret for long, and soon journalists were making inquiries. During this time, Neilia gave birth to a daughter, Naomi, on November 8, 1971. It wasn't until March of 1972 that Biden finally went public with his candidacy.

Biden's campaign strategy was to build the voters' trust. He felt people's faith in politicians had eroded over the years. Biden built trust by being blunt with his opinions and the policies he supported. He was fond of saying, "You may not agree with me, but at least you'll know where I stand."[1] Biden was against the Vietnam War (1954–1975) and blamed President Richard Nixon for escalating the conflict rather than ending it. Biden supported civil rights, women's rights, and environmental issues.

A lack of money was always an issue for Biden's campaign. To make up for it, Biden and his campaign staff recruited an army of volunteers, who made phone calls and went house-to-house throughout the state handing out flyers. The money Biden's campaign was able to raise was spent on radio ads and campaign literature.

Week by week, Biden crept up in the polls. Ten weeks from the election, he and Boggs were even. When it appeared that Biden might actually win, the race began getting national attention. Republicans became worried and began pouring more resources into Boggs's campaign. Vice President Spiro Agnew even came to Wilmington to rally support. But Biden was also able to pull in outside support, including visits from Senator Edward Kennedy and vice presidential candidate Sargent Shriver.

On the evening of the election, Biden situated himself in a suite on the tenth floor of Wilmington's

EIGHTEEN TO VOTE

The 1972 election was the first national election after the ratification of the Twenty-Sixth Amendment to the Constitution, which lowered the voting age from 21 to 18. As part of his campaign strategy, Biden visited numerous high schools to court young voters. He also hoped that students might pass along his message to their parents and influence their votes.

Hotel du Pont. The lead went back and forth throughout the night, but at 10:30, Biden led Boggs by 2,600 votes. A little after midnight, his sister Val announced to a crowd gathered in the hotel ballroom, "We won!"[2] The official tally was 115,528 to 112,542.[3] Biden had pulled off the greatest political upset in Delaware history.

Tragedy Strikes

Biden had a lot to do before the Senate convened in January. He had to search for a place for him and his family to live in Washington, DC, find schools for his two sons, and get a babysitter for one-year-old Naomi. He also had to hire his senatorial staff. On December 18, Biden and his sister took the train to Washington to conduct staff interviews. That afternoon, Biden's brother Jimmy called from Wilmington and asked to speak to Val. When she hung up the phone, Biden noticed she looked pale. "There's

Biden, Neilia, and their kids celebrated his thirtieth birthday soon after the election, on November 20, 1972.

been a slight accident," she said, and she advised that they return to Wilmington.[4]

While Biden was in Washington, Neilia had gone shopping with their kids. As she was crossing an intersection in her station wagon on the way home, they were hit by a semitruck, throwing the car into a row of trees. Neilia and Naomi were killed instantly. Four-year-old Beau broke many bones, and three-year-old Hunter suffered a fractured skull. When Biden reached the hospital, a doctor told him that his sons were in fair condition but that Hunter's head injury could result in permanent brain damage.

Biden was beside himself with grief over the loss of his wife and daughter. In his 2007 memoir, he described his feelings in the first moments at the hospital: "I could not speak, [I] only felt this hollow core grow in my chest, like I was going to be sucked inside a black hole."[5] Biden stayed with his sons for days, only leaving for his wife's and daughter's memorial service. He threw himself into the minute-by-minute needs of his sons as a way to cope with the pain.

Two weeks before he was due to be sworn into the Senate, Biden called Senate majority leader Mike Mansfield and told him he would not be taking his Senate seat. Afterward, Mansfield and Minnesota senator Hubert Humphrey called Biden almost every day to convince him to change his mind. Mansfield put Biden on the Senate Steering Committee, which assigned senators to various committees and set priority for legislation—an unheard-of appointment for a new senator. Mansfield told Biden he was needed for several important Steering Committee votes. "Give me six months, Joe," Mansfield said.[6] Biden's family and friends also tried to convince him to take his Senate seat,

Biden took his oath of office at the hospital where his boys were recovering.

insisting that Neilia would have wanted it as well. When Biden learned that his sons would make full recoveries, he finally agreed to give the Senate a try for six months.

Senator Biden

On January 3, 1973, the recently elected senators took the oath of office on the floor of the House of Representatives, but Biden wasn't among them. He refused to leave his sons even for such an occasion, so the Senate passed a special resolution allowing Biden to take his oath from the hospital. Two days later, in the chapel of the Wilmington Medical Center, Biden was sworn in by Senate secretary Frank Valeo. Biden's father-in-law held the Biden family Bible on which the new senator placed his left hand. Biden's sons watched from a hospital bed, which had been wheeled into the chapel for the occasion. Biden spoke briefly afterward, saying, "I hope I can be a good senator for you all."[7] But he affirmed that he would give up his Senate seat the moment it prevented him from being a good father.

In his earliest days in the Senate, Biden saw himself as an observer. He assumed that his first two years would be primarily a learning experience, but his colleagues saw to it that he was kept busy. Biden was assigned to the Banking, Housing, and Urban Affairs Committee and the Public Works Committee. Biden's Senate colleagues went out of their way to make him feel welcome. They invited him out to lunch and to the Senate gym, but Biden often refused. He had little interest in getting to know his colleagues at the time. He had bouts of depression, and he spent the entirety of some days alone in his office. He would later say, "Losing Neilia and Naomi had taken all the joy out of being a United States senator; it had taken all the joy out of life."[8] Members of his staff took bets on how long he would last before he quit.

Once both of Biden's sons were released from the hospital, his sister Val moved in with them and helped take care of the boys during the day while he was in Washington. Each night Biden would make the trip back to Wilmington, either by car, train, or airplane, to put his sons to bed. He was in constant contact with them while he was away, and he even had a mobile phone installed in his car so he could talk to them while he drove. Over time, as he and his sons became accustomed to the routine, Biden became more at ease being away from home and more confident as a senator. He began accepting lunch and party invitations from his colleagues, and he started doing speaking engagements and fundraisers. When Biden reached the six-month mark, he told a reporter for the Wilmington *Evening Journal*, "I'm probably going to stay the whole term."[9]

AMTRAK JOE

Biden liked to use the passenger rail service Amtrak to travel between his home in Wilmington and Washington, DC, and over the years he made the trip as many as 8,000 times, earning him the nickname Amtrak Joe. A reporter for Wilmington's *News Journal* called Amtrak "the symbol of his political career."[10] Biden got to know the Amtrak employees well. In a 2009 interview, Biden said, "The folks who work on the train have become like family to me."[11] In appreciation for his years of loyalty, Amtrak officials named the Wilmington station the Joseph R. Biden Jr. Railroad Station in 2011.

CHAPTER
FIVE

AN AMBITIOUS SENATOR

As time passed after his wife's death, Biden became more active in the Senate and discovered he loved being a senator. In his first two years, he was a vocal supporter of impeaching President Richard Nixon over Watergate, a scandal in which the president's administration covered up its involvement in a break-in at the Democratic National Committee headquarters. Biden also worked to benefit his home state and improve the lives of his constituents. He clamped down on pollution in Delaware cities, asked for additional federal drug enforcement agents in the state, and fought to enlarge Cape Henlopen State Park, located on the state's southeastern coast.

As a senator, Biden's ambition was to be on the Foreign Relations Committee. This is one of the most prestigious committees in the Senate, and it deals with matters related to foreign policy, such as treaties, foreign

During his time in the US Senate, Biden regularly commuted home to Delaware in the evenings to be with his children.

economic and military aid, and declarations of war. In 1975, while still a freshman senator, Biden was assigned to the committee. Biden had always been interested in foreign affairs, and being assigned to the Foreign Relations Committee meant he finally had the chance to help influence them. In 1978, Biden was assigned to the Judiciary Committee, which oversaw the Department of Justice.

"A Real Gentleman"

One evening in March 1975, as he was waiting for his brother Frank to pick him up at the Wilmington airport, Biden spotted an advertisement for the New Castle County parks system that featured an attractive young woman. When his brother arrived, he pointed out the ad and told his brother, "That's the type of girl I'd like to date."[1] To Biden's surprise, his brother said he knew her from the University of Delaware, and Frank gave him her phone number. Biden called her the next day. The woman who answered the phone was Jill Tracy Jacobs. Biden introduced himself and asked her whether she was available to go out that evening, but she said she already had a date. Biden said he was only in town for

Jill worked as a teacher, and later in life she earned a doctoral degree in education.

one day and asked her if she would break off the date. She agreed.

At dinner that evening, Biden learned that Jacobs had no interest in his work, so they talked about everything but politics. Jacobs was 24 years old and a student at the University of Delaware. She was in the process of divorcing her husband, whom she had married when she was 18, and she wasn't looking for a long-term relationship. But looking back years later, Jill would recall, "He was laid-back and funny. . . . It was a much better date than I had expected it to be."[2] After Biden dropped her off at home, Jacobs called her mother and told her, "I've finally met a real gentleman."[3]

While dating, Biden asked Jacobs to marry him several times, but she kept saying no. She was not yet ready to join the tight-knit Biden family, help raise two young boys, and deal with the publicity of being married to a senator. After dating for two years, Jacobs finally agreed, and the two were married on June 17, 1977. Jill became close with Beau and Hunter. She took them to school and after-school events, prepared their meals, and took care of them when they were sick. In time, they came to see her as a mother. On June 8, 1981, Jill gave birth to a daughter, Ashley.

A Run for President

Twice, Democrats approached Biden to run for president, once for the 1980 election and again for the 1984 election. They thought his youth would attract votes. But Biden wasn't yet ready for such a significant leap and rejected the notion. He saw 1988 as his first real opportunity to run for president. He would have more than a decade of experience in politics to draw on by then, and with President Ronald Reagan's second term coming to an end, there would be no incumbent to run against that year. But it wouldn't be an easy election. Biden lacked national recognition, and his voter base came from the second-smallest state in the country. Biden's greatest accomplishments up to that point included being chair of the Senate Judiciary Committee and leading a debate on the strategic arms limitation treaty with the Soviet Union. Political analysts and journalists questioned whether that was enough.

Biden officially announced his candidacy in June 1987. Standing before a crowd of supporters in front of the Wilmington Amtrak station, he spoke of the need to improve the education and welfare of American children, saying, "This is the issue upon which I will stake my candidacy."[5] This was an unusual subject for a presidential candidate to run on, but Biden believed that making it about children would give his campaign purpose and would set him apart from the other candidates.

The first hiccup in Biden's campaign came just a few weeks after he declared his candidacy. Chief Justice Lewis Powell announced his retirement from the Supreme Court, and President Reagan nominated Robert Bork as his successor. As chair of the Senate Judiciary Committee, Biden presided over the nominee review process. Not only did this take him away from his campaign but Biden received bad press for publicly opposing Bork before his confirmation hearing even began. Then, in September, his voters' trust took a hit.

On September 12, the *New York Times* published an article about a speech Biden gave at the Iowa State Fair the month before. In the speech, he had quoted British Labour Party leader Neil Kinnock and failed to give him credit. This prompted the media to look back throughout Biden's campaign and career for other cases of plagiarism. Journalists found other instances in which Biden quoted Robert F. Kennedy and Hubert Humphrey without giving attribution. The *New York Times* also

Biden's run for president drew a lot of attention, but scandals surrounding plagiarized portions of speeches caused the campaign to fizzle.

published a story on Biden's law school plagiarism incident. The final blow came when *Newsweek* published an article outlining a campaign event at which Biden exaggerated his academic achievements. These events eroded peoples' confidence in Biden and threatened to derail his campaign. Biden publicly admitted his plagiarism and exaggerations were due to sloppiness, and he said that no deception had been intended. Numerous colleagues came to Biden's defense, but the damage had been done, and on September 23, Biden withdrew from the 1988 presidential race.

Back to Business

Biden immediately returned to the Bork hearings, which he called "the most significant Supreme Court nomination in the last several decades."[6] Biden opposed Bork's nomination as a Supreme Court justice, not because he wasn't qualified but because Bork's views on civil rights and women's rights differed significantly from his own. Bork had served as acting attorney general, a US court of appeals judge, and a professor of law at Yale University. Biden tried something unprecedented in the history of Senate judicial confirmations: he used Bork's ideology as a basis for rejection. Biden and his staff combed through Bork's past and dug up numerous instances where he had been critical of court decisions upholding civil rights, free speech, reproductive rights, and the separation of church and state.

Biden wrote regarding Bork years later: "As a judge he would not recognize fundamental human rights

At a hearing Biden held up a stack of letters from legal scholars opposing Bork's nomination to the Supreme Court.

beyond what was spelled out in the Constitution."[7] In Biden's view, this was unacceptable for a Supreme Court justice, and many other senators felt the same. After three weeks of hearings, the Senate rejected Bork's appointment 58–42.[8] The event was a turning point for the Senate. Experience was no longer the sole qualification for a presidential appointee. From then on, one's personal history and ideology would be a significant factor.

Health Crises

Biden was typically a healthy person, but in early 1987 he began suffering from headaches. His friends, family, and staff suggested they were probably due to stress from overworking. But when his presidential campaign and the Bork hearings ended, his headaches remained. Then, in February 1988, the pain intensified. After being rushed to the hospital following a debilitating episode, doctors discovered a ruptured blood vessel, or aneurysm, at the base of his brain. Biden needed surgery to repair the damage before it got worse, so he was transported to the Walter Reed National Military Medical Center near Washington, DC. Doctors there ran additional tests and discovered a second, smaller aneurysm on the opposite side of his brain. After the surgery he spent ten days recuperating at the hospital.

Not long after returning home, Biden began suffering from severe chest pain. He was rushed to the hospital again, where doctors discovered a blood clot in his lung. Biden spent ten days in the hospital undergoing tests and having a filter installed in his artery that would catch any additional clots before they reached his heart or lungs.

In May, Biden returned to Walter Reed, where doctors successfully repaired his second, smaller aneurysm. Biden didn't return to the Senate until September, seven months after first being admitted to the hospital. His entire family accompanied him on his first day back and watched from the Senate gallery as senators unanimously passed a resolution welcoming him back and gave him a standing ovation. Afterwards, several senators stood and spoke in tribute, including Republican senator Bob Dole, who said: "To the surprise of no one who knows Joe Biden's spirit and tenacity . . . he triumphed."[9]

Proudest Moments

Biden worked on various pieces of crime legislation while a member of the Senate Judiciary Committee. In 1990, Biden began preliminary work on the Violence Against Women Act (VAWA) after learning that violent crimes against women were on the rise. The law was eventually enacted as part of

BIDEN AND PUBLIC SAFETY

In his 2007 memoir, Biden asserted that protecting Americans was the first duty of the government, and he said it was one that he took seriously. He wrote: "A government must ensure safe homes, streets, schools, and public places before it can fulfill any other promises."[10]

the Violent Crime Control and Law Enforcement Act in 1994. Among its provisions, the VAWA provided grants for law enforcement training, violent crime research, victim counseling, and women's shelters. It also provided restitution guidelines and created the National Domestic Violence Hotline. Biden would later look back on the VAWA as one of his proudest accomplishments.

Another of Biden's proudest accomplishments was his role in the Balkans after the breakup of Yugoslavia. In the early 1990s, the various republics that made up the southeastern European country of Yugoslavia, which is part of a region called the Balkans, began splitting apart. Violence soon erupted between rival factions. Biden became interested in these events when, as chair of the Senate Subcommittee on European Affairs, he was contacted by refugees from the conflict who

LGBTQ RIGHTS

Biden's views on LGBTQ rights changed over time. In 1993, he voted in favor of the military's don't ask, don't tell policy, which allowed people who identified as LGBTQ to serve in the military only if they kept their orientations secret. In 1996, he voted in favor of the Defense of Marriage Act, which prevented government recognition of same-sex marriages. However, in 2010, he supported the repeal of the don't ask, don't tell policy, and he became a public supporter of same-sex marriage in 2012. He officiated the marriage of a same-sex couple in 2016.

told him about the atrocities being committed in the region. Biden began holding hearings in 1991, but his Senate colleagues had little interest in getting involved in the Balkans at the time. It wasn't until August 1992 that the full extent of the atrocities came into view. Serbians, under the leadership of Slobodan Milosevic, were committing genocide against Muslims in Bosnia and creating a humanitarian crisis.

Biden supported the idea of military strikes and sanctions against the Serbs, but it took three years of escalating violence in the Balkans, and Biden's persistent arguing for intervention, before the Senate agreed to act. In July 1995, the Senate voted to remove an arms embargo that had deprived Bosnians of the means to defend themselves. Then in August, forces from the North Atlantic Treaty Organization (NATO), led by the United States, began bombing the Serbs in Bosnia. This quickly forced Milosevic to seek a peace agreement. Biden had been crucial in promoting awareness of events in the Balkans and steering US and international policy to put an end to the violence in the region. During the conflict, more than 140,000 people were killed and millions were displaced.[11]

Iraq

In 2002, President George W. Bush took an aggressive posture toward Iraq. Bush's intelligence agencies indicated that Iraq was stockpiling weapons of mass destruction and posed an imminent threat to the United States and its allies. In late July 2002, Biden held a hearing in the Senate Foreign Relations Committee to examine the threat posed by Iraq. What he learned

9/11

For Biden, the morning of September 11, 2001, started out like most mornings—riding the Amtrak from Wilmington to the capital. But thirty minutes into his commute he heard that a plane had crashed into the North Tower of the World Trade Center in New York City. By the time he arrived in Washington, a second plane had hit the South Tower and a third had hit the Pentagon building. This left no doubt in his mind that an orchestrated terrorist attack was in progress.

The Senate building had been evacuated, so Biden and his colleagues met in a building near the Senate offices and held a briefing. Biden suggested returning to work in order to show the public that the government was still in control, but officials decided that was too dangerous. There were rumors of additional airplanes headed for Washington. Unable to help, Biden decided to return to Wilmington, but outside the Senate office building he was approached by a reporter eager for news from government officials. Biden gave an interview in an effort to help reassure the American people. He concluded the interview by saying, "This nation is too big, too strong, too united, too much a power in terms of our cohesion and our values to let this break us apart, and it won't happen."[12]

Biden initially supported the use of force against Iraq, a Senate decision that led to the US invasion of Iraq in 2003.

was that Iraq's nuclear program was years away from having a viable weapon, and therefore the country posed little threat.

Bush advocated for an aggressive response if Iraq didn't comply with UN weapons inspectors, but he needed approval from the Senate in order to carry out that response. Bush asked the Senate for expansive powers to deal with Iraq, including the use of force. Some senators, including Biden, considered his request overreaching. They were eventually able to work out a joint resolution that gave the president most of what he wanted, but with strict Senate oversight. With Biden's support, the joint resolution was approved on October 16, 2002. When diplomatic efforts failed to compel Iraq president Saddam Hussein to submit to weapons inspections, Bush ordered the invasion of Iraq in March 2003. Biden would come to regret supporting the joint resolution and would fight to repeal it. He considered the Iraq invasion premature, and he criticized Bush for not garnering enough foreign support and for not having a clear post-invasion strategy.

Biden the Author

In 2007, Biden published an autobiography called *Promises to Keep: On Life and Politics.* He ended the book with a positive outlook for the future of the United States, saying:

> I see a future in which Americans remember that when we value what we hold in common above all else, there is nothing we cannot achieve. We won't do it as blacks or as whites, as southerners or northerners. We won't do it as rich or as poor, as men or as women—we won't even do it as Democrats or as Republicans—but as a people of faith, together, listening to our own best voice.[13]

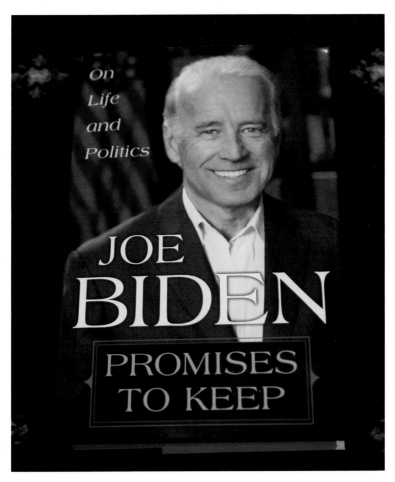

Biden's first book, *Promises to Keep*, summed up his life and career so far, but higher offices still awaited him.

The book made it onto the *New York Times* best seller list. But it wasn't a complete story. There was still more in store for Biden.

CHAPTER
SIX

OBAMA/BIDEN '08

Few people doubted that Biden would run for president again after he dropped out of the 1988 race. His next best opportunity was the 2008 election. He was confident his extensive foreign policy experience would clinch him the Democratic nomination. By that time, Biden was in his sixth term in the Senate and was up for reelection for a seventh in 2008.

Campaigning had changed since Biden's last presidential bid. Instead of reading newspapers and tuning into nightly radio and television news programs to learn about candidates, many voters turned to the internet and comedy news shows on cable TV. Biden did his best to keep up with the trends. His official campaign kickoff day in January 2007 included an appearance on *The Daily Show* with Jon Stewart, which aired on the Comedy Central network.

Early national polls put Biden behind senators Hillary Clinton and Barack Obama. Biden did well on the debate stage, but he was never able to raise the kind

Biden and Barack Obama leave a December 2007 Democratic primary debate.

of money that Obama did, and he didn't have Clinton's name recognition. He failed to rise in the polls. After finishing fifth in the Iowa caucuses, Biden dropped out of the race in January 2008. Obama eventually triumphed in the Democratic primaries.

The Short List

After Biden dropped out of the presidential race, rumors began circulating that he could be chosen as Obama's vice president. Some people saw a natural chemistry and respect between the two during their presidential debates. Biden was, in fact, on Obama's short list of candidates along with Clinton. Obama didn't just want a running mate whose popularity would boost his election campaign. He wanted a person who would be an active vice president and adviser. When Obama asked Biden whether he would consider being his vice president, Biden said he had to think about it. Biden and Obama did not know each other well. Obama had only been a senator for a few years before running for president. Biden had also publicly stated on several occasions that he didn't want to be vice president and said that he was happy being chair of the Senate Foreign Relations

Committee. Biden believed he could have more political influence in that role.

Biden eventually agreed to be vetted by Obama's campaign staff in consideration for vice president, but he wouldn't commit until he could speak to Obama in person to discuss their visions of what the vice president's role would be in an Obama administration. This meeting occurred in a hotel in Minneapolis, Minnesota, on August 6, 2008. During their late-night

BARACK OBAMA

Barack Obama got involved in Democratic politics while working as a lawyer in Chicago, Illinois. He was elected to the Illinois Senate in 1996 and the US Senate in 2004. Obama's rise to fame began after he gave an inspiring keynote speech at the 2004 Democratic National Convention, which some political scholars consider to be one of the greatest political speeches of the twenty-first century.

In his first year in the US Senate, Obama was assigned to the Foreign Relations Committee, where Biden was the ranking Democrat. Obama and Biden were uncertain of each other at first. Biden was leery of Obama's ambition, charisma, and quick rise to fame. Obama saw Biden as old-fashioned, and he found Biden's long speeches tiresome. But Obama learned to respect Biden on the presidential primary debate stage, where Biden's extensive experience and political knowledge were plain to see. After Biden withdrew from the 2008 presidential race, Obama called him on numerous occasions. Biden later recalled it was "not so much to ask for advice as to bounce things off me."[1] Over time, the two came to be close friends.

Biden and Obama meet with voters at an Illinois rally in August 2008.

talk, Biden laid out his conditions: "If you're asking me to join you to help govern, and not just help you get elected, then I'm interested," he said. "I don't want to be a vice president who is not part of the major decisions you make."[2] Obama agreed. On August 23, Obama publicly introduced Biden as his vice presidential pick at a campaign event in Springfield, Illinois. On August 27, Obama and Biden were officially nominated for president and vice president at the Democratic National Convention.

Biden had many ups and downs during the months between the nomination and the election. Many media outlets praised him after he was nominated for vice president, but they also criticized him for his many verbal gaffes, including telling supporters at a campaign event in New Hampshire that Hillary Clinton was more qualified than him to be vice president. He also forgot people's names and job titles on multiple occasions. These gaffes allegedly strained his relationship with Obama, who assigned two staffers to travel with Biden to rein him in. As the election drew near, Biden began using a teleprompter more often when campaigning for Obama, and he avoided the press as much as possible.

The Election

Obama began Election Day ahead in the polls against his Republican rival, Arizona senator John McCain. Obama

"JOE BOMBS"

Biden was known for speaking offhand, which led to frequent slipups, or gaffes. *Newsday* called him "gaffe-a-minute Joe."[3] Biden's own staff called his slips "Joe bombs."[4] Some were offensive, such as when he described presidential candidate Barack Obama as a "mainstream African American, who is articulate and bright, and clean" in a 2007 call with reporters.[5] But most gaffes were harmless accidents. Some people appreciated that Biden spoke his mind rather than from written speeches. Obama campaign staffer David Wade said in 2008, "It would be a huge mistake to try and strip away the authenticity that's been [Biden's] greatest strength for 35 years."[6]

was seen as a catalyst for change in America, while McCain was expected to continue the agenda of his predecessor, President George W. Bush. At the end of the day, the American people voted for change. Obama won the election with 365 electoral votes against McCain's 173. Obama also won the popular vote with 69.5 million votes compared to McCain's 59.9 million.[7] In his victory speech that night, Obama thanked Biden for his help during the campaign, saying: "I want to thank my partner in this journey, a man who campaigned from his heart and spoke for the men and women he grew up with on the streets of Scranton and rode with on that train home to Delaware, the Vice President-elect of the United States, Joe Biden."[8]

On January 20, 2009, Biden walked across the southern steps

Supreme Court justice John Paul Stevens administered the oath of office to Biden.

of the US Capitol to take the oath of office. His wife, Jill, held the family Bible on which he placed his left hand. With his sons Beau and Hunter and his daughter Ashley standing nearby, Biden raised his right hand and took the oath, becoming the forty-seventh vice president of the United States. The event was the culmination of almost 40 years in politics that saw Biden rise from county councilman to the second-highest office in the country.

CHAPTER
SEVEN

VICE PRESIDENT BIDEN

Before Biden agreed to be Obama's vice president, he requested to be present at important meetings and to be part of the decision-making process. He wanted to be an adviser, not a bystander. This fit with Obama's vision for his vice president, and he agreed to Biden's request. President Obama kept his word. Biden was given an office in the West Wing of the White House and frequently attended Obama's daily intelligence briefings and other meetings. Biden had regular access to the president, and the two even shared a private lunch together once a week.

The first thing on the agenda of the new administration was to overcome the financial crisis that was gripping the country after the collapse of the housing market and subsequent failures of several major banks. Obama signed the American Recovery and Reinvestment Act of 2009, which provided hundreds

Biden speaks with National Security Adviser Susan Rice in the Oval Office of the White House while Obama discusses policy with Iraqi officials.

of billions of dollars to individuals, companies, and government programs to help stimulate the economy. Obama put Biden in charge of oversight of the stimulus money to make sure it was used appropriately with as little waste as possible. Biden assembled a team of financial experts to help. He was in regular contact with various state and federal officials who spent the money, and he traveled the country to personally see it being put to use. His efforts paid off. Later analysis found that only around one percent of the nearly $800 billion in stimulus funds was wasted.[1]

The next issues facing the Obama administration were the ongoing war in Afghanistan and the withdrawal of US troops from Iraq. Biden's years of experience on the Senate Foreign Relations Committee made him an ideal person to offer advice from a nonmilitary point of view. Just weeks before their inaugurations, Obama sent

WORKING FOR THE MIDDLE CLASS

Obama made Biden chair of the White House Task Force on the Middle Class in 2009, which was tasked with raising the living standards of the middle class. Biden and task force members traveled the country promoting ways to accomplish this goal, which included creating jobs in the manufacturing industry, improving retirement security, increasing childcare assistance, and making higher education more affordable.

Biden to Afghanistan and Iraq to assess the situations there. Biden supported the war in Afghanistan, but he was against sending more troops—a view contrary to that of Obama's military advisers. Instead, Biden advised fine-tuning military strategy in Afghanistan using the forces already on the ground and ramping up the training of local Afghan forces. Obama eventually sided with his military advisers and agreed to send additional troops to Afghanistan, but he made some concessions based on Biden's advice, such as setting a specific date on which to withdraw the troops and using them to combat terrorists rather than to rebuild the country.

Obama also put Biden in charge of overseeing the effort to reconcile the various ethnic and religious groups in Iraq in the hopes of creating stability in the country after the withdrawal of US forces. Biden traveled to Iraq in July and September of 2009 to discuss the issue with Iraqi officials, but he was unable to create much change before the US troop withdrawal in 2011 put an end to his efforts. Biden would later refer to Iraq as "the most frustrating issue of my forty-year career in foreign relations." He explained, "Relations among the three main factions in Iraq—Shia Arabs, Sunni Arabs, and Kurds—were characterized by anger

Biden meets with US troops in Iraq in July 2009.

and paranoia, and punctuated by spasms of outright violence. The three factions nursed grudges both ancient and modern."[2]

A Second Term

Biden was nominated for a second term as vice president at the 2012 Democratic National Convention. He and Obama went on to win that year's election against former Massachusetts governor Mitt Romney and Wisconsin congressman Paul Ryan. But Biden's second term would not go as smoothly as his first.

Biden made the news several times in 2015 for making unwanted physical contact with women and young girls at various political events. At Senator Chris Coon's swearing in ceremony in early 2015, Biden whispered into the ear of Coon's 13-year-old daughter and attempted to kiss the side of her head. Then at the February swearing in ceremony of Obama's new secretary of defense, Ashton Carter, photos showed Biden placing his hands on the shoulders of Carter's wife, Stephanie, and whispering in her ear. Biden's actions were harshly criticized by the media and on social media, where some people began calling him Creepy Uncle Joe, while acquaintances and supporters brushed the incidents aside as just "Biden being Biden."[3] Stephanie Carter later wrote that in her view, Biden hadn't done anything wrong: "The Joe Biden in my picture is a close friend helping someone get through a big day, for which I will always be grateful."[4] While Biden didn't speak about the incidents at the time, he began to take a more public stance against sexual harassment. In November of 2015, Biden published an op-ed in university newspapers around the country on stopping sexual assaults on campuses, and in February

BURISMA HOLDINGS

In 2014, Biden was part of the US diplomatic effort to help Ukraine following a revolution that overthrew the country's government. Shortly after Biden got involved, his son Hunter joined the board of directors of the Ukrainian natural gas company Burisma Holdings. The White House rejected claims that there was a conflict of interest, because Hunter was a private citizen and Biden would not be endorsing Burisma.

Part of Biden's job was to encourage the Ukrainian government to root out corruption. In 2016, he pressured the government to fire its top prosecutor, Viktor Shokin, who was seen as being too soft on politicians who were accused of corruption. Biden even threatened to withhold $1 billion in US aid to Ukraine unless Shokin was fired. News soon broke that Shokin had once led an investigation into Burisma for corruption, leading some to believe that Biden had gotten Shokin fired to protect his son. However, evidence indicated that Shokin's Burisma investigation was inactive at the time he was fired, which cast doubt on Biden's alleged motive. In February 2020, Ukraine launched an investigation into Biden's role in Shokin's firing.

of 2016, he spoke about consent and sexual abuse at the 88th Academy Awards.

Another Run?

By the fall of 2014, people had begun asking questions about whether Biden would run for president again in 2016. Biden had reasons not to. At the time, his eldest son, Beau, was suffering from a relapse of brain cancer that he had been treated for a year earlier. Beau was 45 years old and had followed in his father's footsteps to become a lawyer and politician. He was also an officer in the Delaware National Guard who had served in Iraq. Biden was reluctant to commit to running for president, even though Beau and the rest of his family had given their approval. He wanted to help Beau through his illness and support Beau's ambition to run for governor of Delaware after he recovered. In the spring of 2015, Beau's condition worsened. When the public noticed that his son hadn't been seen at several important political events, Biden made a public announcement that Beau was undergoing treatment at the Walter Reed National Military Medical Center.

On May 30, 2015, Beau died at the age of 46, surrounded by his family at Walter Reed. Biden was devastated, but staying busy was one way he dealt with grief. He was back at work only four days after Beau's funeral. When he returned to his office, he had more than 70,000 letters of condolence waiting for him.[5] In October, Biden officially announced that he would not be running in the 2016 presidential election, stating that the window of opportunity had closed during the grieving process.

Biden eventually endorsed Hillary Clinton for president and aided her campaign. Clinton's Republican rival was businessman and television personality Donald Trump. He ran an unconventional campaign. Critics said Trump encouraged violence at campaign rallies.[6] They also said he used racial stereotypes.[7] But Trump's bombastic personality, bluntness, and America-first policies won over many Americans. Biden often spoke out against what he saw as Trump's lack of morals. "[Trump] does not have the basic fundamental sensibilities and values that almost every American politician, left, right and center, I know, have," Biden said at a Clinton campaign event in September 2016.[8] Trump went on to win the presidential election that November.

Biden threw his support behind Hillary Clinton's 2016 campaign for the presidency.

Life After the White House

In January 2017, as the Obama administration neared its end, President Obama held a farewell press conference for Biden. Obama commended Biden's foreign affairs work and his role as presidential counselor. Afterward, Obama surprised Biden by awarding him with the Presidential Medal of Freedom, the nation's highest civilian honor. "With his charm, candor, unabashed optimism and deep and abiding patriotism," the award citation read, "Joe Biden has garnered the respect and esteem of colleagues of both parties and the friendship of people across the nation and around the world. . . .

Biden became emotional as President Obama surprised him with the Presidential Medal of Freedom.

A grateful nation thanks Vice President Joseph R. Biden Jr. for his lifetime of service."[9]

Biden's term as vice president ended on January 20, 2017. Afterward, he created several nonprofit organizations to continue his public service. These included the Biden Foundation, the Biden Cancer Initiative, and the Biden Institute at the University of Delaware. He was also named the Benjamin Franklin Presidential Practice Professor at the University of

Pennsylvania, and he was put in charge of the university's new Center for Diplomacy and Global Engagement. These organizations worked to stop violence against women, aided cancer research, and promoted the study of diplomacy and foreign policy.

ACCUSATIONS

In early 2019, several women came forward with stories of being touched inappropriately by Biden in the past. Among those was former Biden staffer Tara Reade, who said he used to put his hands on her shoulders and run his fingers along her neck when she worked for him in 1993. Reade later said Biden had sexually assaulted her. Biden denied assaulting Reade. The *New York Times* and the *Washington Post* conducted investigations into the allegation but found no evidence of an assault. Reade said she filed a written complaint at the time, but a record of that complaint did not surface.

CHAPTER
EIGHT

AN ATYPICAL CAMPAIGN

On April 25, 2019, Biden released a video announcing his campaign to run against incumbent president Donald Trump. In the video, Biden denounced Trump, saying that the president had frequently lied to the public, promoted racism, and put his own interests over those of the country. "The core values of this nation, our standing in the world, our very democracy, everything that has made America, America, is at stake," Biden said in the video. "That's why today I'm announcing my candidacy for President of the United States."[1]

When Biden entered the 2020 presidential race, there were already more than a dozen Democratic candidates, including senators Bernie Sanders, Elizabeth Warren, and Amy Klobuchar, and South Bend, Indiana, mayor Pete Buttigieg. Biden's name recognition made him an instant front-runner for the Democratic

Biden launched his campaign for president in April 2019, more than a year and a half before the election.

nomination, but he placed a disappointing fourth in the Iowa caucus and fifth in the New Hampshire primary. It looked like Biden was set to lose his third presidential nomination attempt, and Sanders became the new front-runner. However, Biden made a huge comeback, winning South Carolina in February and ten states

THE TRUMP IMPEACHMENT

Shortly after Biden announced his candidacy, Trump sent his personal lawyer, Rudy Giuliani, to Ukraine to look into Biden's connection to the investigation of natural gas company Burisma and the firing of Ukrainian prosecutor Viktor Shokin in 2016. Then Trump in a July 25 phone call personally asked Ukrainian president Volodymyr Zelensky to investigate Biden. In addition, Trump withheld congressionally approved military aid to Ukraine. Trump said that by doing these things, he was fighting corruption in Ukraine. He accused Biden of misusing his position as vice president to help Burisma, which his son was involved with. Trump's inquiry, the administration said, was carried out under an international agreement for cooperation in criminal investigations. Critics argued that he was actually trying to undermine Biden's campaign.

The House of Representatives launched an impeachment inquiry into Trump's actions, which ended on December 18, 2019, with Trump being impeached on two counts: one count of abuse of power for soliciting foreign aid to influence the outcome of the 2020 presidential election, and one count of obstruction of Congress for refusing to cooperate with the impeachment inquiry. Trump became the third president in US history to be impeached. An impeachment trial was held in the Senate. If the Senate voted to convict him, he would be removed from office. If the Senate voted to acquit him, he would remain in office. The Senate voted to acquit.

during the Super Tuesday primaries on March 3. CNN called it the "biggest, fastest and most unexpected comeback in modern political history."[2] Then, everything changed.

The Coronavirus

In early 2020, a virus that had been discovered in Wuhan, China, late the previous year began spreading around the world. It was a type of virus called a coronavirus, and scientists named the disease it caused COVID-19. Most people who contracted COVID-19 recovered, but some became very ill and died from the disease. The disease was especially dangerous to older people and those with preexisting health conditions. At age 77, Biden was at high risk of developing a severe illness, so on March 11 he formed a committee of medical experts to advise his campaign on how to stay safe during the pandemic. On their recommendations, Biden canceled numerous public events, and he began hosting virtual meetings from his Wilmington home. But Biden's campaign didn't have a well-developed virtual presence, and it struggled as his staff tried to modernize. During his first virtual event—a town hall meeting on March 13—the sound was garbled and the video cut out after only four minutes. Other events would suffer similar problems.

Biden left home for a debate against Sanders on March 15. Meeting on the debate stage in Washington, DC, Biden and Sanders bumped elbows instead of shaking hands. This had become a socially acceptable way to greet people during the pandemic to avoid spreading the virus. In a room without an audience, standing behind podiums spaced a safe distance apart, the two discussed their proposed responses to the coronavirus at great length before moving on to more typical topics such as immigration and education.

By the end of March, most states had issued mandatory stay-at-home orders to slow the spread of the virus. People were asked to leave their homes only for essential reasons. These orders affected around 300 million Americans by early April.[3] Biden was no exception, so he turned the basement of his Wilmington home into a campaign headquarters, where he spent up to seven hours a day on the phone with his campaign staff, advisers, and donors. But Biden's isolation meant his campaign wasn't getting national coverage, while Trump had extensive media coverage as president. Trump had begun giving daily coronavirus updates,

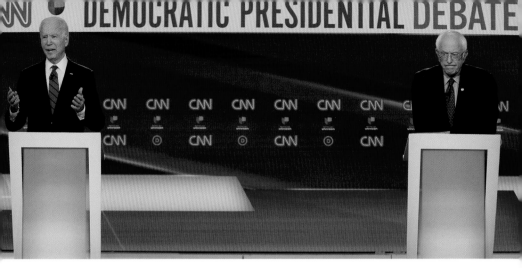

Vermont senator Bernie Sanders was Biden's last major rival in the Democratic primaries.

which also provided opportunities to promote his policies. Biden needed a way to compete, so he had a television studio set up in his basement where he could continue to be seen and heard during his campaign. He also launched a podcast called *Here's the Deal* to broadcast discussions on important issues with experts.

On April 8, Sanders ended his campaign. By then, Biden had won nine additional states, making a Sanders comeback highly unlikely. With Sanders out, Biden became the presumptive Democratic nominee, and on June 5, he obtained the 1,991 delegates needed to officially clinch the nomination.[4]

In early May, President Trump began traveling the country again, often visiting swing states that would be key to his reelection. But Biden chose to remain in lockdown. It wasn't until May 25—Memorial Day—

that Biden left his home for a public event. Donning a face mask, he laid a wreath at a veterans' memorial in New Castle, Delaware. Afterward, Biden began making regular public appearances using recommended safety measures, but on June 30, he announced that he would not be holding any public campaign rallies.

Surpassing Trump

In June, Biden led Trump in the polls.[5] By then, many Americans had become critical of Trump's handling of the coronavirus pandemic. The death toll in the United States crossed 100,000 in late May, a total far higher than in other countries, and continued rising. Extended lockdowns had dealt a blow to the economy, too, causing millions to lose their jobs. Trump was also reprehended for what critics called callous behavior during the nationwide civil unrest following the May 25 death of George Floyd. Floyd was a Black man who died in Minneapolis, Minnesota, after a white police officer knelt on his neck for around eight minutes.

When protests and riots sprang up across the country, Trump said he could send in the military and tweeted, "When the looting starts, the shooting starts."[6] Then, on June 1, Trump had peaceful protesters dispersed with tear gas so he could walk to a church across the street from the White House. The following day, Biden denounced Trump at a campaign event in Philadelphia, saying, "The president is more interested in power than in principle. . . . His narcissism has become more important than the nation's well-being."[7]

AN EMOTIONAL RESPONSE

After the death of George Floyd, Biden traveled to Floyd's hometown of Houston, Texas, to speak with his family in person. He also spoke at Floyd's funeral service. He spoke via video link so he and his Secret Service bodyguards wouldn't draw attention away from Floyd. In his emotional broadcast, Biden said, "Now is the time for racial justice . . . because when there is justice for George Floyd, we will truly be on our way to racial justice in America."[8]

CHAPTER
NINE

THE 2020 ELECTION

As the Democratic National Convention approached in August, Americans were anxious to see whom Biden would choose as his running mate. The vice president was not only a crucial member of a president's administration but could also give the presidential candidate a boost in polling numbers and campaign funds at a critical time in a campaign. In a March presidential debate, Biden had said he would choose a woman as his vice president in order to make his administration more diverse.

After much deliberation, Biden chose California senator Kamala Harris. Harris was a popular figure in the Democratic Party. She had run in the Democratic primaries for the 2020 presidential nomination, and she was someone who, according to Biden, had "enormous strength."[1] Harris, who was 22 years younger than Biden and of Jamaican and Indian ancestry, could potentially broaden the ticket's appeal to young voters and voters of color.

Kamala Harris joins Biden at an Arizona campaign event in October 2020.

The Final Stretch

In September, Biden escalated his attacks against Trump, blaming him for the civil unrest that characterized the summer of 2020. Biden also blamed Trump for failing to contain the coronavirus and for the subsequent death of hundreds of thousands of Americans. When a February recording surfaced in September in which Trump stated he had knowingly downplayed the pandemic earlier in the year, Biden responded harshly, saying: "He had the information. He knew how dangerous it was. . . . He failed to do his job on purpose. It was a life and death betrayal of the American people."[2] Trump defended his response to the pandemic, saying, "I don't want people to be frightened. I don't want to create panic. . . . We want to show confidence. We want to show strength."[3]

The Biden and Trump campaigns agreed to three in-person debates, the first of which took place on September 29. Both candidates stood on a stage while a moderator presented each with a series of questions. The debate quickly turned chaotic. Trump frequently interrupted Biden and insulted him and his family. Some analysts believed Trump was trying to provoke Biden into making mistakes that Trump could use against him.

Biden, Trump, and the moderator spoke loudly to be heard over one another, making it difficult to discern what was being said. Biden frequently looked into the camera and spoke directly to the American people to get his messages across, but he also sparred with Trump at times, calling him a "clown," and "the worst president America's ever had." At one point, Biden responded to an interruption from Trump by saying, "Will you shut up, man?"[4] The *New Yorker* called it the "worst debate in American history" and a "national humiliation."[5]

Shortly after, the Commission on Presidential Debates (CPD), which sets rules for presidential debates,

THE BIDEN PROBE

In August 2019, Senate Republicans began an investigation of the Bidens' dealings in Ukraine while Biden was vice president. Their goal was to determine whether Biden used his position as vice president to help the natural gas company Burisma, which his son Hunter was associated with. They charged that this would have been an abuse of power. Democrats viewed the investigation as a ploy by Republicans to hurt Biden's presidential campaign. Republican senator Ron Johnson, who led the investigation, appeared to confirm in an August interview that this would be one result of such an investigation, saying, "I would think it would certainly help Donald Trump win reelection."[6] The results of the investigation were released on September 23. Investigators found no evidence of wrongdoing by the Bidens. A spokesperson for Biden's campaign called the investigation "an attack founded on a long-disproven, hardcore right-wing conspiracy theory."[7]

The first debate was held at Case Western
Reserve University in Cleveland, Ohio.

announced that it would change the format of the second
debate to reduce the number of interruptions. The
Trump campaign rejected the idea of changing the rules.
To some, the prospect of further presidential debates
seemed doubtful.

Then, in early October, Trump tested positive for
the coronavirus. He recovered after a brief hospital
stay, but as a precaution the CPD announced that the
second debate would be a virtual event. While Biden
agreed to attend a virtual debate, Trump refused, and
the CPD canceled the event. Instead, Biden and Trump

held competing town hall–style events in which they answered questions from voters.

Biden and Trump finally met in person for another debate on October 22. This time, the rules were different. When a candidate gave his opening remarks on a new question, the other candidate had his microphone turned off. This prevented the kind of interruptions seen during the first debate. The result was a much more subdued discussion.

A Historic Election

The 2020 election was unlike any before. Because of the pandemic, millions of people voted by mail. Many felt unsafe going to voting locations in person. Preelection polls suggested Biden had an advantage, but people on both sides anxiously awaited

Election Day. To get the 270 electoral college votes he needed to win, Biden had to win in several key swing states. These are states with no clear front-runner. They included Arizona, Florida, Michigan, North Carolina, Pennsylvania, and Wisconsin. Trump had won all of those states in 2016, and Biden had worked hard during his campaign to win over their voters.

Election Day was November 3, but because so many mail-in ballots had to be counted, many expected a winner to be determined after several days. By the end of Election Day, Biden was ahead in electoral votes. But results in key swing states were still close and uncertain. Most of the remaining ballots to be counted were mail-in ones, and Biden was expected to gain more votes from them. For months, Trump had discouraged mail-in voting, and people voting for Biden were much more likely to use the vote-by-mail option.

As the mail-in votes trickled in over the next few days, Biden surpassed Trump's vote totals in several states. Trump called for some states to stop counting ballots. His campaign and other groups filed lawsuits claiming voter fraud. Trump said thousands of ballots were cast after the election and therefore illegal. The counting continued, and the lawsuits were later

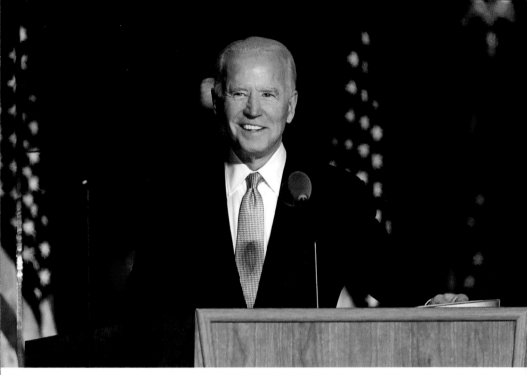

Biden gave his victory speech on the night of
November 7 in Wilmington, Delaware.

dismissed. Several major news organizations projected
on November 7 that Biden was the president-elect of the
United States. Biden had won Pennsylvania, putting him
over the 270 electoral votes he needed to win.

That night, Biden spoke to the American people
from his hometown of Wilmington. He said: "My fellow
Americans, the people of this nation have spoken. They
have delivered us a clear victory. A convincing victory. A
victory for 'We the People.'"[9] In achieving this victory,
Biden had fulfilled his boyhood goal of being elected
president. Now, he began his effort to unite a divided
nation as the forty-sixth president of the United States.

TIMELINE

1942
Joseph Robinette Biden Jr. is born on
November 20 in Scranton, Pennsylvania.

1957
In September, Biden begins attending school at
Archmere Academy in Claymont, Delaware.

1965
Biden graduates from the University
of Delaware in the spring.

1966
On August 27, Biden marries Neilia Hunter.

1969

Joseph R. "Beau" Biden III is born on February 3.

1970

Hunter Biden is born on February 4. In November, Biden is elected as a New Castle County councilman.

1971

Naomi Biden is born on November 8.

1972

Biden is elected to the US Senate in November. In December, his wife and daughter are killed in a car crash.

TIMELINE

1977
On June 17, Biden marries Jill Tracy Jacobs.

1981
Ashley Biden is born on June 8.

1987
In June, Biden announces he is running for president in the 1988 election, but he withdraws on September 23.

1988
Biden undergoes surgery to repair an aneurysm in February and again in May.

2007
In January, Biden announces he is running for president in the 2008 election.

2008
Biden drops out of the presidential election in January; he later becomes Barack Obama's running mate, and the Obama-Biden ticket is elected in November.

2009

As vice president, Biden helps oversee the stimulus spending passed to help the country out of a recession. Drawing on his experience in foreign policy, he advises President Obama on military moves in Iraq and Afghanistan.

2017

In January, President Obama awards Biden the Presidential Medal of Freedom, the nation's highest civilian honor.

2019

On April 25, Biden announces he is running for president against incumbent Donald Trump.

2020

Biden accepts the Democratic presidential nomination on August 20. On November 3, he is elected the forty-sixth president of the United States.

ESSENTIAL FACTS

Date of Birth
November 20, 1942

Place of Birth
St. Mary's Hospital, Scranton, Pennsylvania

Parents
Joseph R. Biden Sr. and Catherine Finnegan Biden

Education
University of Delaware
Syracuse University College of Law

Marriage
Neilia Hunter (1966–1972)
Jill Tracy Jacobs (1977–)

Children
Joseph "Beau," Hunter, Naomi, Ashley

Career Highlights
Biden began a long political career at the age of 30 after a short but successful career as a lawyer. He rose to become a prominent senator for the state of Delaware and became vice president in 2008. He was elected forty-sixth president of the United States in 2020.

Societal Contributions

As a senator, Biden helped pass the Violence Against Women Act, designed to improve the investigation and prosecution of violent crimes committed against women. As vice president, he oversaw the American Recovery and Reinvestment Act, which helped boost the economy after a major recession.

Conflicts

While in law school in 1965, Biden committed plagiarism by not properly citing a source in a writing assignment. In 2007, he described senator Barack Obama as a "mainstream African American, who is articulate and bright, and clean," which many people saw as a racially insensitive comment. In 2015 and 2019, several women accused Biden of touching them inappropriately in the past.

Quote

"If you entrust me with the presidency, I will draw on the best of us, not the worst. I will be an ally of the light, not of the darkness."—*Joe Biden, 2020 Democratic National Convention*

GLOSSARY

acquit
To clear a person of the charges that have been brought against him or her.

aneurysm
The weakening and bulging of an artery wall.

compulsive
Having powerful urges to do something.

convention
A gathering of members of a political party that meets to select a candidate to run for office.

delegate
A person sent to a political convention to represent a candidate, group, or state.

drafted
Selected for mandatory military service.

extemporaneous
Done with little or no advanced preparation.

gaffe
A mistake, especially one that's widely noticed.

pandemic
The worldwide spread of a disease.

plagiarism
The act of copying and claiming another person's words or ideas as your own.

primary
A contest political parties hold to determine their presidential nominees.

resolution
A formal opinion or decision made, usually after voting, by a legislature or other group.

stimulus
Something that prompts further activity.

ADDITIONAL RESOURCES

Selected Bibliography

Biden, Joe. *Promises to Keep: On Life and Politics*. Random House, 2007.

"Joe Biden: Who He Is and What He Stands For." *New York Times*, 31 Aug. 2020, nytimes.com. Accessed 1 Sept. 2020.

"Joe Biden's DNC Speech." *CNN Politics*, 21 Aug. 2020, cnn.com. Accessed 1 Sept. 2020.

Further Readings

Allen, John. *The Trump Presidency*. ReferencePoint, 2020.

Henzel, Cynthia Kennedy. *Voting Issues of Today*. Abdo, 2021.

Streissguth, Tom. *The 2016 Presidential Election*. Abdo, 2018.

Online Resources

To learn more about Joe Biden, please visit **abdobooklinks.com** or scan this QR code. These links are routinely monitored and updated to provide the most current information available.

Places to Visit

Democratic National Committee
430 South Capitol St. SE
Washington, DC 20003
202-863-8000
democrats.org
The official website of the Democratic Party features information about the party, its political positions, and its organizations and initiatives across the country.

The White House
1600 Pennsylvania Ave. NW
Washington, DC 20500
202-456-1111
whitehouse.gov
The official website of the White House features information about the building's history, how it is used today, and how to plan a tour.

SOURCE NOTES

Chapter 1. Light in the Darkness

1. Jacob Pramuk. "Read Joe Biden's Full 2020 Democratic National Convention Speech." *CNBC*, 21 Aug. 2020, cnbc.com. Accessed 29 Sept. 2020.

2. Derrick Bryson Taylor. "A Timeline of the Coronavirus Pandemic." *New York Times*, 6 Aug. 2020, nytimes.com. Accessed 29 Sept. 2020.

3. Allison Prang and Jennifer Calfas. "U.S. Coronavirus Deaths Top 173,000." *Wall Street Journal*, 20 Aug. 2020, wsj.com. Accessed 29 Sept. 2020.

Chapter 2. A Natural Leader

1. Jules Witcover. *Joe Biden: A Life of Trial and Redemption*. HarperCollins, 2010. 14.

2. Joe Biden. *Promises to Keep: On Life and Politics*. Random House, 2007. 18.

3. Biden, *Promises to Keep*, 4.

4. Biden, *Promises to Keep*, 4.

5. Norm Lockman. "Boggs vs. Biden: A Tough Tussle." *News Journal*, 24 Oct. 1972, newspapers.com. Accessed 29 Sept. 2020.

Chapter 3. Finding His True Calling

1. Joe Biden. *Promises to Keep: On Life and Politics*. Random House, 2007. 25.

2. Jules Witcover. *Joe Biden: A Life of Trial and Redemption*. HarperCollins, 2010. 41.

3. Biden, *Promises to Keep*, 65.

4. Biden, *Promises to Keep*, 28.

5. Witcover, *Joe Biden*, 57.

6. Biden, *Promises to Keep*, 50.

7. "State of Delaware Official Results of General Election, 1970." *State of Delaware*, 1970, elections.delaware.gov. Accessed 12 Oct. 2020.

Chapter 4. Victory and Loss

1. Joe Biden. *Promises to Keep: On Life and Politics*. Random House, 2007. 65.

2. Terry Zintl and Norm Lockman. "State Elects the Youngest U.S. Senator." *Evening Journal*, 8 Nov. 1972, newspapers.com. Accessed 1 Oct. 2020.

3. Jules Witcover. *Joe Biden: A Life of Trial and Redemption*. HarperCollins, 2010. 106.

4. Biden, *Promises to Keep*, 79.

5. Biden, *Promises to Keep*, 79.

6. Biden, *Promises to Keep*, 82.

7. Norm Lockman. "TV Newsman Draws Second Oath from Biden." *Morning News*, 6 Jan. 1973, newspapers.com. Accessed 1 Oct. 2020.

8. Biden, *Promises to Keep*, 88.

9. John Schmadeke. "Biden Probably Will Finish His Term." *Evening Journal*, 11 June 1973, newspapers.com. Accessed 1 Oct. 2020.

10. Celia Cohen. "Democrats and Republicans Say Delaware Stands by Biden." *News Journal*, 24 Sept. 1987, newspapers.com. Accessed 1 Oct. 2020.

11. Nancy Doyle Palmer. "Joe Biden: 'Everyone Calls Me Joe.'" *Washingtonian*, 1 Feb. 2009, washingtonian.com. Accessed 1 Oct. 2020.

Chapter 5. An Ambitious Senator

1. Jill Biden. *Where the Light Enters: Building a Family, Discovering Myself*. Flatiron Books, 2019. 45.

2. Biden, *Where the Light Enters*, 46.

3. Biden, *Where the Light Enters*, 47.

4. Pat Ordovensky and Richard Sandza. "Biden Punctures '84 Presidential Boomlet," *Morning News*, 13 Aug. 1980, newspapers.com. Accessed 1 Oct. 2020.

5. Robert Shogan. "Biden in Race, Cites Difficult Path to Future," *Los Angeles Times*, 10 June 1987, latimes.com. Accessed 1 Oct. 2020.

6. Kenneth B. Noble. "Biden Vows to Lead Forces against Bork's Confirmation," *New York Times*, 9 July 1987, nytimes.com. Accessed 1 Oct. 2020.

7. Joe Biden. *Promises to Keep: On Life and Politics*. Random House, 2007. 178.

8. Biden, *Promises to Keep*, 211.

9. Biden, *Promises to Keep*, 234.

10. Biden, *Promises to Keep*, 239.

11. "Transitional Justice in the Former Yugoslavia." *International Center for Transitional Justice*, 2009, ictj.org. Accessed 1 Oct. 2020.

12. Jason Ryan. "9/11 Flashback: Biden Called for Resilience, Warned about Civil Liberties in War on Terror." *ABC News*, 11 Sept. 2011, abcnews.go.com. Accessed 1 Oct. 2020.

13. Biden, *Promises to Keep*, 364.

Chapter 6. Obama/Biden '08

1. Jules Witcover. *Joe Biden: A Life of Trial and Redemption*. HarperCollins, 2010. 482.

2. Ryan Lizza. "Biden's Brief." *New Yorker*, 13 Oct. 2008, newyorker.com. Accessed 1 Oct. 2020.

3. Christopher Beam. "How Joe Biden Became Gaffe-Proof." *HuffPost*, 25 Oct. 2008, huffpost.com. Accessed 1 Oct. 2020.

4. Mark Leibovich. "For a Blunt Biden, an Uneasy Supporting Role." *New York Times*, 7 May 2012, nytimes.com. Accessed 1 Oct. 2020.

5. Shane Croucher. "Joe Biden's Biggest Gaffes: Quotes, Blunders That Could Hurt a 2020 Presidential Campaign." *Newsweek*, 9 Feb. 2019, newsweek.com. Accessed 1 Oct. 2020.

6. John M. Broder. "Biden Living Up to His Gaffe-Prone Reputation." *New York Times*, 11 Sept. 2008, nytimes.com. Accessed 1 Oct. 2020.

7. "2008 Presidential Popular Vote Summary." *Federal Election Commission*, 2008, fec.gov. Accessed 1 Oct. 2020.

8. "Full Transcript: Sen. Barack Obama's Victory Speech." *ABC News*, 4 Nov. 2008, abcnews.go.com. Accessed 1 Oct. 2020.

9. Joe Biden. "Sen. Joe Biden's Farewell Speech to the Senate." *RealClearPolitics*, 15 Jan. 2009, realclearpolitics.com. Accessed 1 Oct. 2020.

SOURCE NOTES CONTINUED

Chapter 7. Vice President Biden

1. All Things Considered. "A Look Back at How Joe Biden Managed the 2009 Stimulus Package." *NPR*, 6 Apr. 2020, npr.org. Accessed 1 Oct. 2020.

2. Joseph R. Biden Jr. *Promise Me, Dad: A Year of Hope, Hardship, and Purpose.* Flatiron Books, 2017. 136.

3. Associated Press. "Just Joe Being Joe? Biden's Odd Moments Give Pause." *Denver Post*, 17 Feb. 2015, denverpost.com. Accessed 1 Oct. 2020.

4. William Cummings. "Wife of Ex-Defense Secretary Defends Biden, Says Viral Photo Used 'Misleadingly.'" *Delaware Online*, 1 Apr. 2019, delawareonline.com. Accessed 1 Oct. 2020.

5. Biden, *Promise Me, Dad,* 204.

6. Libby Cathey and Meghan Keneally. "A Look Back at Trump Comments Perceived by Some as Inciting Violence." *ABC News*, 30 May 2020, abcnews.go.com. Accessed 12 Oct. 2020.

7. Z. Byron Wolf. "Trump's Attacks on Judge Curiel Are Still Jarring to Read." *CNN*, 27 Feb. 2018, cnn.com. Accessed 12 Oct. 2020.

8. Arlette Saenz. "Joe Biden Slams Donald Trump's Comment That Housing Crisis Was 'Good Business.'" *ABC News*, 27 Sept. 2016, abcnews.go.com. Accessed 1 Oct. 2020.

9. Melissa Chan. "Read the Full Transcript of President Obama Surprising Joe Biden with the Medal of Freedom." *Time*, 12 Jan. 2017, time.com. Accessed 1 Oct. 2020.

Chapter 8. An Atypical Campaign

1. Alexander Burns. "Joe Biden's Campaign Announcement Video, Annotated." *New York Times*, 25 Apr. 2019, nytimes.com. Accessed 1 Oct. 2020.

2. Stephen Collinson. "Joe Biden's Historic and Unbelievable Political Comeback Dominates Super Tuesday." *CNN*, 4 Mar. 2020, cnn.com. Accessed 1 Oct. 2020.

3. Jason Silverstein. "43 States Now Have Stay-at-Home Orders for Coronavirus. These Are the 7 That Don't." *CBS News*, 6 Apr. 2020, cbsnews.com. Accessed 1 Oct. 2020.

4. Scott Detrow. "Biden Formally Clinches Democratic Nomination, While Gaining Steam against Trump." *NPR*, 5 June 2020, npr.org. Accessed 1 Oct. 2020.

5. "2020 Election Forecast." *FiveThirtyEight*, 12 Oct. 2020, fivethirtyeight.com. Accessed 12 Oct. 2020.

6. Barbara Sprunt. "The History Behind 'When the Looting Starts, the Shooting Starts.'" *NPR News*, 29 May 2020, npr.org. Accessed 12 Oct. 2020.

7. "Read: Joe Biden's Remarks on Civil Unrest and Nationwide Protests." *CNN*, 2 June 2020, cnn.com. Accessed 1 Oct. 2020.

8. Adam Edelman. "Biden Calls for 'Racial Justice' during Emotional George Floyd Funeral Speech." *NBC News*, 9 June 2020, nbcnews.com. Accessed 14 Oct. 2020.

Chapter 9. The 2020 Election

1. "Transcript: Joe Biden, Kamala Harris' First Joint Interview with ABC's Robin Roberts." *ABC News*, 23 Aug. 2020, abcnews.go.com. Accessed 14 Oct. 2020.

2. "Joe Biden Speech Transcript Warren, Michigan September 9." *Rev*, 9 Sept. 2020, rev.com. Accessed 14 Oct. 2020.

3. Jeremy Herb and Kevin Liptak. "White House and Trump Campaign Scramble to Respond to Woodward Revelations." *CNN*, 9 Sept. 2020, cnn.com. Accessed 15 Oct. 2020.

4. "Read the Full Transcript from the First Presidential Debate between Joe Biden and Donald Trump." *USA Today*, 4 Oct. 2020, usatoday.com. Accessed 14 Oct. 2020.

5. Susan B. Glasser. "'This Is So Unpresidential': Notes from the Worst Debate in American History." *New Yorker*, 30 Sept. 2020, newyorker.com. Accessed 14 Oct. 2020.

6. Kyle Cheney. "Besieged on All Sides, Ron Johnson Says His Probe 'Would Certainly' Help Trump Win Reelection." *Politico*, 13 Aug. 2020, politico.com. Accessed 14 Oct. 2020.

7. "Senator Ron Johnson's US-Ukraine Investigation Released." *CBS 58*, 23 Sept. 2020, cbs58.com. Accessed 14 Oct. 2020.

8. John Verhovek. "Biden Campaign Expands Legal Team in Preparation for Voting Fight in November." *ABC News*, 14 Sept. 2020, abcnews.go.com. Accessed 14 Oct. 2020.

9. "Read: President-Elect Joe Biden's Full Victory Speech." *Yahoo! News*, 7 Nov. 2020, news.yahoo.com. Accessed 9 Nov. 2020.

INDEX

ABOUT THE AUTHOR

Ryan Gale

Ryan Gale is a Minnesota-based artist and writer with a passion for US history and learning about the nation's many diverse people.

ABOUT THE CONSULTANT

Rachel Blum, PhD

Rachel Blum, PhD, is a political science professor at the University of Oklahoma in the Department of Political Science and the Carl Albert Congressional Research and Studies Center. Her research focuses on political parties in the United States, and she is the author of *How the Tea Party Captured the GOP: Insurgent Factions in American Politics*. She completed her PhD in government at Georgetown University in 2016.